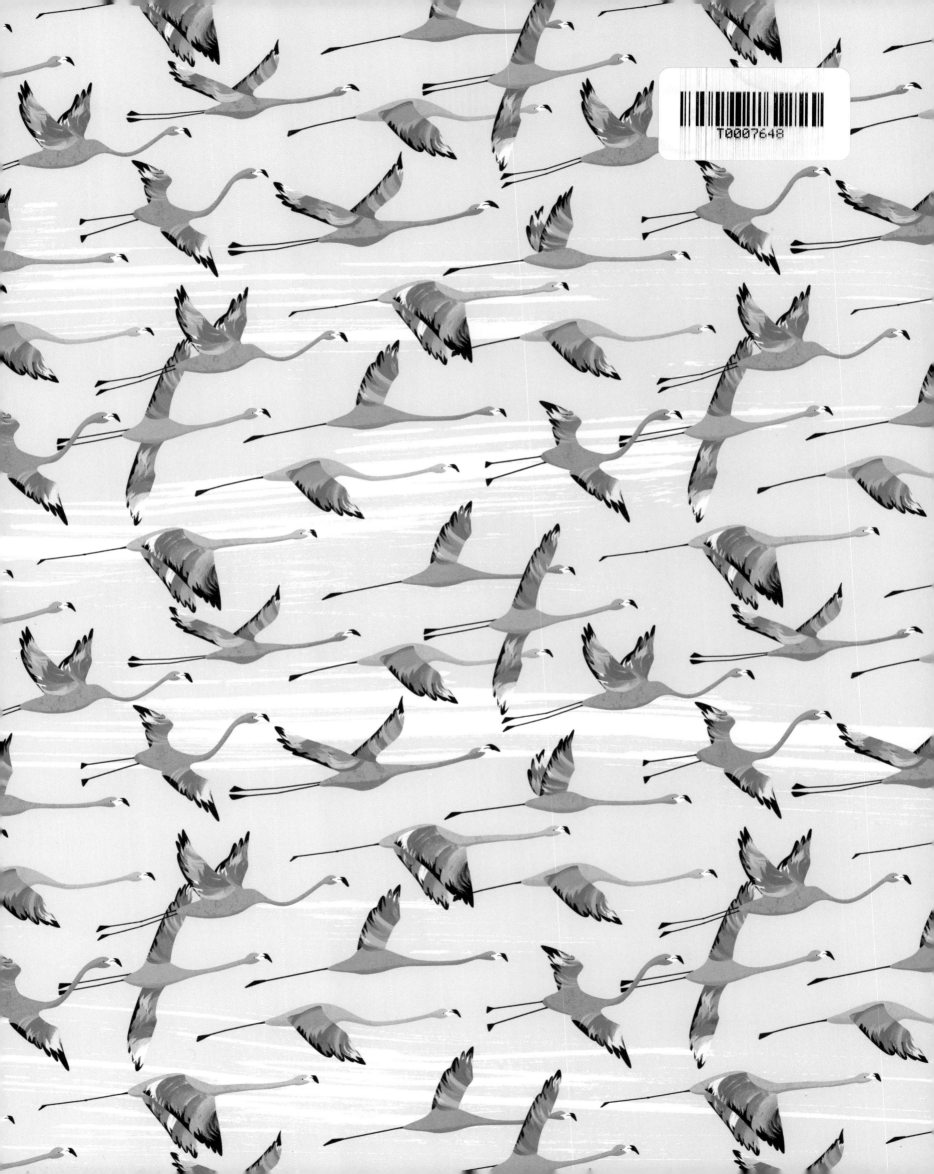

Published in 2022 by Orange Mosquito
An Imprint of Welbeck Children's Limited
part of Welbeck Publishing Group.

Based in London and Sydney.

www.welbeckpublishing.com

To my parents, Justo and Marga, for sharing their love of art and teaching me the value of effort. TÀNIA

Design and layout © Mosquito Books Barcelona, SL 2020
Text © Mia Cassany 2020
Illustration © Tània Garcia 2020
Translated by Howard Curtis
Publisher: Margaux Durigon
Production: Clare Hennessy

ISBN: 9781914519383
eISBN: 9781914519390

Printed in China

10 9 8 7 6 5 4 3 2 1

FSC
www.fsc.org
MIX
Paper from
responsible sources
FSC® C020056

No animals were harmed in the making of this book, but a few were bribed into helping out.

ANIMALS: TOGETHER OR ALONE

A crash of rhinos, a waddle of penguins and other fun facts

MIA CASSANY · TÀNIA GARCIA

ORANGE
M·O·S·Q·U·I·T·O

Fun names of groups of animals:

A bloat of hippos

A crash of rhinos

A flamboyance of flamingos

A horde of mandrills

A waddle of penguins

An aurora of bears

A clutter of spiders

A bed of scorpions

A dazzle of zebras

A pod of dolphins

A mob of kangaroos

A hive of bees

This book reveals special and surprising facts about how animals interact with each other. In it, you will find very sociable creatures who live in groups numbering more than a hundred: like a hive of 50,000 bees who carefully share and coordinate daily tasks. And then there are animals who spend most of their lives alone: like the solitary octopus in the middle of a huge ocean, who rarely socializes with others of its species.

However, even the most solitary animal in the world isn't always on its own; during periods of mating it will seek a partner and, in some cases, abandon its solitude to look after its eggs or young.

Be amazed by the enormous diversity of the animal world: each species has distinct characteristics and so acts in a different way with other members of its same species.

How can it be that some animals need a group to survive while others can make it on their own? You'll learn the answers to this intriguing question in the pages of this unique book.

Read on to discover and be wowed by the fascinating contrasts of the animal kingdom. . . .

Hippopotamus

The case of the very curious hippopotamus . . . Hippos congregate in large herds of up to 100 animals at a time—but even so, many scientists don't think of them as being sociable animals. It is thought that hippos gather in places where there is enough food and water to support them and not because they form strong social bonds.

Each hippo lives as an individual, taking care of its needs while surrounded by other members of the same species. The only caring relationships that develop within the group are between mothers and their calves. Scientists have done a great deal of research into the behavior of these groups as it is highly unusual for solitary animals to want to be together. Most scientists think hippos gather like this out of habit, since staying together in a large group doesn't bring them any individual disadvantages.

Rhinoceros

Most rhinos are solitary and very territorial animals. Animals who are this protective of their own space and intolerant of intruders have little desire to mix with other animals—even of their own species. If these animals live in communities or groups, it is out of necessity: either because predators lie in wait, and many eyes are better at spotting danger than just two, or because they can't hunt alone. However, none of these reasons apply to the rhinoceros. Rhinos are herbivores and don't need to hunt. They are huge animals and their bodies are among the strongest in the world, so there aren't many predators they need to worry about. Of the five distinct species of rhino that exist, the white rhino is slightly more sociable—even though they still react with surprising aggression to the proximity of any other animal, except for their own calves.

Flamingo

Flamingo colonies usually have between fifty and 20,000 members. The size of the group depends on how much space they are surrounded by. If there are no boundaries in their environment, it is very possible for the group to grow to an enormous size—there are colonies in Africa with more than a million flamingos! Not all the flamingos in a group are related, but there are familial subgroups within the larger group. The colonies are well organized and have a leader, who reminds everyone that it is in command by constantly stretching its neck. A curious thing about flamingos is that they march together in almost perfect synchronicity: walking very close to each other, at the same speed and in the same direction. Of course, because there are so many of them, it is not a walk that is easy to coordinate. It is the leader who decides when they should start to walk, and also when they should take flight. Flamingos are quite friendly and frequently greet each other by touching wings or rubbing each other lightly.

Golden Eagle

The golden eagle is a majestic, solitary animal of enormous strength and, thanks to its special characteristics, it can easily survive on its own.

Firstly, this majestic bird is highly adaptable to almost all ecosystems; in other words, it is able to live in many parts of the world. Secondly, thanks to its strong legs and sharp claws, the golden eagle is an outstanding, deadly hunter, and it doesn't usually have any problems catching food.

The eagle doesn't need a group to protect and take care of itself as it can fly and hover above trees and cliffs, away from danger. For all these reasons, golden eagles fly solo—living isolated lives. But interestingly, they are also very loyal creatures, as they mate for life. Year after year, during the mating season, golden eagles get together with the same mate for a brief encounter. This is the only time they interact with another of their species.

Mandrill

Mandrills are among the largest primates on Earth. The males are extremely colorful — with incredible purple, blue, and red noses and bright red bottoms. These monkeys live in large groups of between forty and fifty members, although on some occasions they can reach more than six hundred. The groups have very clear hierarchies and each member has specific tasks it must carry out if the group is to function properly. One curious thing about mandrills is that the leader—the dominant male—usually keeps apart from the group. He leads a somewhat solitary life but is always alert to his pack, never losing sight of them and never going too far away in case of danger. Two of the most common behaviors in mandrills are cooperative ones. The first is communication: they "talk" using very loud cries and grunts, which doesn't mean that they are angry; and the second is cleanliness: one of their favorite activities is grooming — when they delouse each other.

Night Monkey

These nocturnal primates are quite cute-looking, with huge round eyes that allow them to see in the dark. They belong to the genus aotus, which means "without ears." They were given this name because when people first started studying them, they couldn't see their ears. Scientists have since discovered that they do have ears but they're hidden by thick fur. Night monkeys live in quite solitary units. When they are young, they find a mate with whom they will live together all their lives—having at most two infants. These families don't mix with any other animals. They spend most of the day resting and sleeping

inside little holes that form in the bark of trees; only coming out at night to eat. Some scientists believe that they keep their families small because there isn't much space in these makeshift homes,

Emperor Penguin

This is the largest penguin in existence and like all species of penguins, it is a flightless aquatic bird. Although it appears clumsy when it walks, the emperor penguin is perfectly adapted for swimming and diving. They are very sociable, and live and hunt in groups. The penguins plunge into the water in a coordinated fashion, diving together and coming back to the surface at the same time, when they have all had a chance to eat. The emperor penguin is very well adapted to the cold, thanks to its very thick plumage and three layers of fat.

However, when temperatures dip as low as they can go, penguins huddle to keep warm and survive. They stand very close together, so as little of their bodies are exposed to the cold as possible. The penguins on the outside swap around with others on the inside; that way, none of them have to stand on the windy cold edges for too long.

These groups are often huge and can have more than a hundred—sometimes thousands!—of members. The penguins protect each other, creating a group defense against the icy weather.

Polar Bear

The polar bear is the largest carnivorous land animal in the world. It certainly doesn't need help hunting! And, thanks to a layer of thick blubber, it doesn't need group warmth either to survive the extremely cold temperatures of the North Pole.

Polar bears only mix with others of their kind when looking for a mate, which happens just once a year. Mothers abandon their solitude to look after their cubs and, most importantly, teach them how to hunt.

In order to make it through their periods of dormancy (a deep sleep) polar bears need to have sufficient stores of fat and energy. If too many polar bears hunt in the same territory, there is less food to go around. Polar bears prefer to live on their own as there is less competition and they have a better chance of surviving.

Very occasionally, small groups of bears have been seen in the same place, but this only really occurs if there is an abundant source of food nearby—such as the carcass of a dead whale. In these cases, the bears coexist for a few days out of self-interest, albeit very cautiously. Bears are not at ease with other bears, and in situations like this they mostly ignore each other.

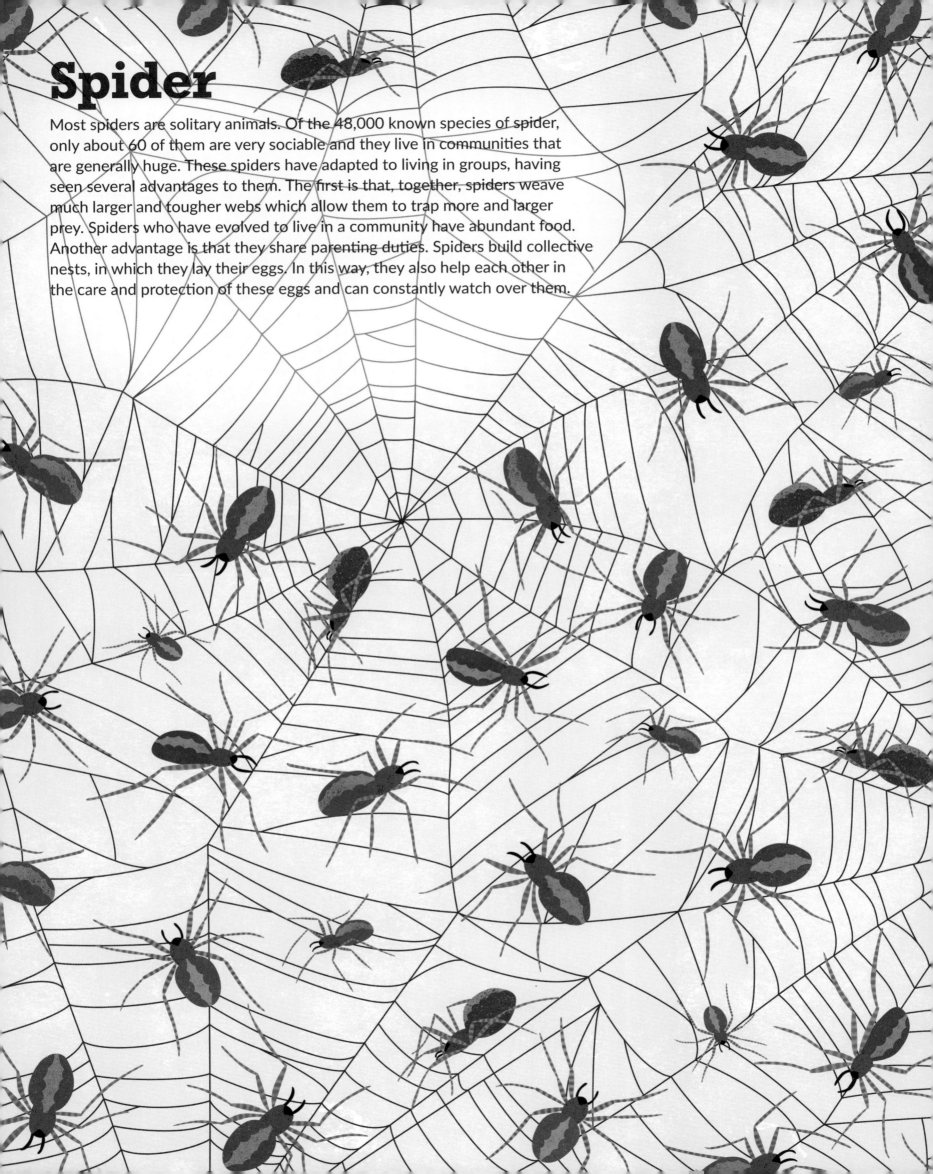

Spider

Most spiders are solitary animals. Of the 48,000 known species of spider, only about 60 of them are very sociable and they live in communities that are generally huge. These spiders have adapted to living in groups, having seen several advantages to them. The first is that, together, spiders weave much larger and tougher webs which allow them to trap more and larger prey. Spiders who have evolved to live in a community have abundant food. Another advantage is that they share parenting duties. Spiders build collective nests, in which they lay their eggs. In this way, they also help each other in the care and protection of these eggs and can constantly watch over them.

Scorpion

Scorpions are extremely solitary animals who only mix when they have to mate. For animals that spend so much time alone, they are good at attracting a mate. They do so by performing a complicated dance routine that has very specific movements, in which they join their pincers. When they have finished mating they separate very quickly. Sometimes, if the male stays close to the female a bit too long, she captures and eats him.

Scorpions are animals with a powerful poison in their stinger, which means there are not many predators—almost none, in fact—who dare to mess with them. So they don't need a pack or a group in order to protect themselves and survive, and they are quite happy to live alone.

Zebra

Zebras are highly sociable animals that live in large groups called a dazzle. They face constant threats from expert predators such as lionesses, so it is vital for zebras to live in a group so that they can protect each other from possible attack. In fact, if a zebra gets separated for even a moment from the group with which it lives, it is very unlikely to stay alive for long.

Groups of zebras are composed of a dominant male, from six to eight females and their foals. Often different dazzles live together, thus creating a larger group that helps them to be more protected. Males that are not yet adult or dominant create their own groups with other unattached males, so that they can protect each other before creating their own dazzle. When attacked, zebras have a particular defense strategy: they gather in a compact group, with the foals in the middle so that no harm comes to them. They stay like that while the dominant male tries to chase away the intruder.

Okapi

Okapis are very shy nocturnal animals about which little is known. They resemble lots of different animals: they have black tongues like giraffes, bodies similar to smaller horses, and a few white stripes like those on zebras. Not only are they solitary animals that don't like company, they are also very timid and elusive; whenever they hear the slightest noise they run away and hide—something they've very good at.

Okapis are so elusive that many well-organized expeditions mounted by scientists to observe and study them haven't even been able to find them. For many years it was believed the okapi were extinct, until in 2006 some specimens were spotted in the Congo. Okapis only get together to mate, and then the mothers raise their calves. Although these animals are very solitary, they are also enormously supportive of others of their species: if a mother okapi dies, another will take over caring for her calf.

Dolphin

These marine mammals may be the most sociable there are on earth. They are known to be highly intelligent animals and many of their behaviors—in communication, problem-solving, interaction—are quite similar to those of humans. Groups of dolphins, known as pods, can consist of four to forty members, and even reach hundreds. Although they are very cooperative and help each other with, for example, hunting, there are hierarchies within the groups. Dolphins organize themselves around these hierarchies and individuals are assigned specific tasks.

If we look carefully at a pod of dolphins, we can easily see that not only do they protect each other and help each other to find food, they also enjoy each other's company. Dolphins play in groups, and even rub their fins together in a kind of caress or give each other provocative little knocks. The group satisfies their need for friendship as well as survival.

Octopus

According to many zoologists, there are few animals more intelligent than octopuses. They are great predators whose highly developed hunting skills mean they obtain all the food they need, on their own. They don't need to form groups, organize or cooperate with other octopuses to get food. In addition, octopuses are experts at hiding — they melt into their surroundings using camouflage to go unnoticed as predators pass by. They don't need groups to protect themselves from possible attack. On the contrary! Swimming alone in the depths of seas and oceans, they are much more difficult to see than if they were in a large group; and they take advantage of this to be more protected. As happens with all animals that don't live in groups, they only look for other octopuses of the same species when it's time to mate, but after this they separate and continue on their way, independently.

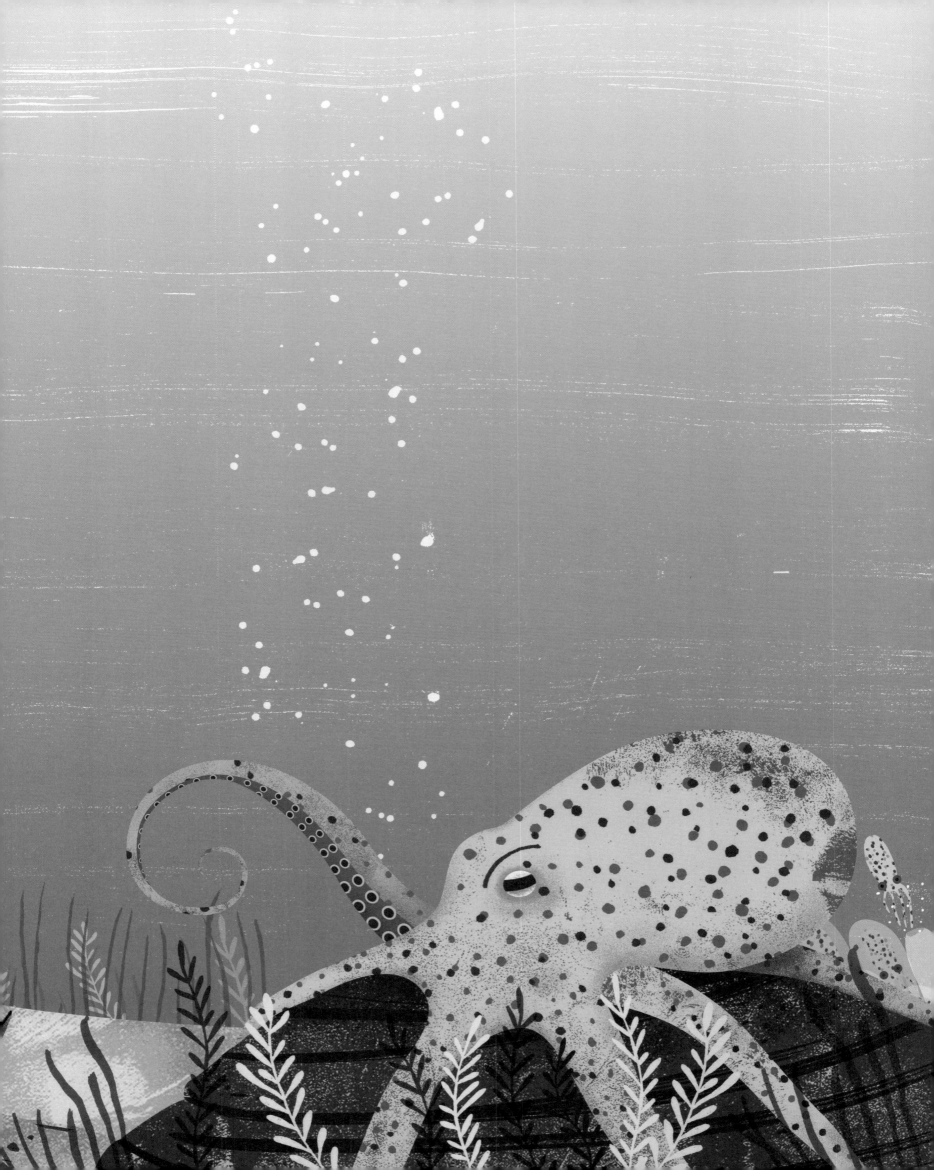

Kangaroo

Kangaroos live in groups called mobs. One of the curious things about mobs is that the number of members varies a great deal depending on the region where they are located—which is why there are communities with a few members and others that are huge. The larger the group, the more the kangaroos mix and the stronger the social structures among the members. Almost all the information kangaroos obtain from other members of the group is through smell. Each kangaroo looks for its own food and eats by itself; they don't need each other in order to forage. But the mobs are essential in protecting each other from predators when they are attacked; being together gives them more chances to survive.

Koala

Koalas are solitary animals who don't like to mix, except when they want to mate or look after their young. The food of the koala is primarily eucalyptus leaves. While they love this plant, it is toxic for most animals, so fortunately they don't need to compete with others for it. All the eucalyptus is for them! Koalas like being alone so much that each one has its own tree, which it marks with specific scratches on the bark to distinguish it. It will only share this tree with its young. Another koala may live in a nearby tree, but never in the same one, so that they don't meet in the branches.
One curious fact about koalas is that if one of them dies, its tree will remain empty for a year and no other koala will live in it during that time.

Bee

Bees are notably social insects. They live in huge communities, called hives,
that can have more than 50,000 members and are organized to perfection.
In order to be able to live with so many others, it is essential that each bee has
a very well-defined task and only they are responsible for carrying it out.
The members of a hive are not equal as there are three social classes in

the hive: drones, workers, and the queen. Bees have distinct physical characteristics that mark their class and correspond to the task required of them. Bees need the group for everything: to feed themselves, to protect themselves, to lay eggs, and to look after their young. A bee without a hive cannot survive.

Mantis

This is a strange animal that really doesn't like the company of its own species, or other animals.
Normally animals that live in groups benefit from being better protected or finding food together.
The mantis doesn't need help with either because it is an expert at camouflage. This creature changes
its normally green color to match its surroundings, cleverly hiding itself from prey and predator.
It doesn't need anyone else to survive and so it avoids contact with other mantises.
When they need to mate, a male and a female mantis will search each other out; but if during this
search two males should be unlucky enough to meet, they will fight until one of them dies.
That's how solitary these insects are!

Curious facts you may not know

- Even though they spend a lot of time in water, hippos cannot swim. They propel themselves along by doing little jumps with their legs.

- A rhinoceros calf can weigh between 90 and 145 pounds at birth, depending on the species. It's one of the heaviest land animals!

- Flamingo chicks are born a gray color, very different from their parents' red or pink plumage. During the first days of life, parents feed chicks with gastric juices. After that, they start to eat crustaceans, and it is this diet that determines the color of their feathers, either a bright red or a pink shade.

- Golden eagles build their nests high up on cliffs, with a base of three thick branches, to which they add sticks and smaller branches. Each year they add a further layer, ending up with nests of enormous size.

- Although mandrill mothers look after their own infants, other females in the group also offer care and affection to infants that are not theirs.

- Every winter, queen bees lay their eggs in cells in a wax honeycomb. From these eggs male and female bees emerge, each with a specific task to do in the hive.

• Mantises only live for a year, in which they change skin six times before they reach adulthood.

• A curious fact about night monkeys is that the female only has one infant a year, which is why, if there are two infants in one of these little families, they will never be the same age.

The infants don't separate from their parents during the first two years of life, which is rather a long time in the animal world.

• The male emperor penguin is in charge of incubating the egg at first, so that the female can feed herself after laying the egg. Later they take turns in looking after the egg.

• The female polar bear digs a shelter-type cave in the ice in which she will spend the dormancy period together with her cubs, feeding them with her milk.

• Spiders lay hundreds of eggs because very few babies, sometimes none, will ever reach adulthood, since they are animals that have a great many predators.

• After 12 months' gestation, the female scorpion can give birth to between two and a hundred infants. When they are born, the first thing they do is climb onto their mother's back so that she can protect them during their first weeks of life, after which she abandons them.

• One curious thing about zebra foals is that when they are born, they "learn" their mother's unique pattern of black and white stripes so that they can distinguish her from other members of the herd.

• Okapis only have one calf a year. The calves cannot distinguish their mother from other females of the same species, which means they can easily be looked after by any female.

• Often, the infant of an animal doesn't resemble its parents at birth. This is the case with emperor penguins or flamingos, for example. Baby dolphins, on the other hand, look exactly the same as their parents, only smaller.

• A female octopus can lay up to 200,000 eggs, but most of them will die in the first two weeks of life.

• Kangaroos and koalas are marsupials, meaning the females have a pouch that covers their teats, in which the babies can safely feed and live for the first months of their lives.